**BEWARE
FALLING TORTOISES**

Also by Sheenagh Pugh

Earth studies and other voyages
Prisoners of Transience (*translations*)

SHEENAGH PUGH

BEWARE FALLING TORTOISES

POETRY WALES PRESS
1987

POETRY WALES PRESS
56 PARCAU AVENUE, BRIDGEND, MID GLAMORGAN

© Sheenagh Pugh, 1987

British Library Cataloguing in Publication Data
Pugh, Sheenagh
 Beware falling tortoises.
 I. Title
 821'.914   PR6066.U42

ISBN 0-907476-70-8

All rights reserved. No part of this publication may be reproduced, stored in a retrieval system, or transmitted in any form or by any means, electronic, mechanical, photocopying, recording or otherwise, without the prior permission of the author.

The cover design by Kevin Perryman incorporates his drypoint 'And brass eternal slave to mortal rage' (c. 1985, the artist), plate size 12.9 × 22.6cm, printed in an edition of 50 copies on Zerkall-Buettn by Max Dunkes, Munich.

Published with the financial support of the Welsh Arts Council

Typeset in 10 point Palatino by Wordsmiths
Printed by Antony Rowe Ltd., Chippenham

Contents

The railway modeller 7
The chess master 8
What a way to go 9
In memory
   1. In Morriston crematorium 11
   2. A matter of scale 12
   3. Reallocation 13
   4. Closing up 14
Magnolia 15
Rockbreaker 16
Eva and the roofers 17
147 19
Snow-blind 20
A short history of cocaine abuse 22
Tulips 23
Sometimes 24
Torturers 25
She was nineteen, and she was bored 26
Penguins at Robben Island 27
Because 28
Babel (1894-1941?) 29
I am Roerek 30
Of the lady whose museum is in Bamburgh 31
Olaf the Quiet 33
Three Epigraphs
  Skeggi 34
  Mary Renault 35
  Epigraph of an impecunious publisher 36
Railway signals 37
Dieppe
   1. Sports Day 39
   2. Finding out 41
   3. Escapers 43
Bad weather 44
Telescope 45

Saga patterns 46
A shipwrecked Inuit learns Gaelic from a Hebridean 47
Framed 49
Memoirs of a Dutch tulip merchant 50
Crusaders
Peat bog burial: Luneberg Heath 54
An even worse way to go 55
Pharisees 56
He was a man of his word 57
A modest request 59
Cameraman 60
Last words of a once proud Lady on her deathbed 61
Rhymes 62

Acknowledgements

Some of these poems have previously been published in *Anglo-Welsh Review*, *Poetry Wales*, *Poets Against Apartheid*, *Contemporary Poems II* (OUP), and the catalogue to Kevin Perryman's exhibition in Munich.

The railway modeller

He's spent all week creating the best part
of a village; sculpting the paper strata
of its hills, painting them green, growing
small metal trees with a teased-out fluff
of foliage. Then he built half-timbered
card houses, secured them where they belonged
and stood back to be sure it was right.

Now he must add the people: so minute,
they take more work than anything. He uses
a make-up brush tapered to a hair
for touching their white plastic into life
with flesh-tones, bright splashes, uniform
blue and grey.... It takes hours to make
an individual, if it's done with love,

but he doesn't mind the time spent
in his shed, a sufficient universe,
and nothing brings a branch line alive
like people. Working down on the track,
picks raised, or waiting on a paper bench
for a train they can't board, they turn
the scene to a frozen photograph.

It's a shame he can't, with all his love,
move the frame on.... The background radio
intrudes news headlines into his thought:
today in Parliament the talking fellows
were voting on whether to punish men
with death. His brush carefully strokes in
blond hair; perfects another passenger.

The chess master

(Karl Schlechter: 1874-1918)

An Austrian master, some said the best,
but never champion; he'd no ambition
to beat the world, and so little taste
for hammering his opponents, that he'd offer
to draw the game from a winning position.

His only title: the drawing master.
It was for him a matter of creating
a pattern, as men may do with number
or music, only in chess it takes two.
It made no sense to talk of defeating

your co-composer, the man who helps you
shape the subtleties. A good game's won
by you and him both; at least he thought so.
Off the board, such a view of the game
was rapidly going out of fashion;

life doesn't offer draws, it would seem,
least of all to so mild a man of sorrows,
and he died rat-poor, while around him
contenders tore the guts out of each other.
He never saw the new world fit for heroes,

(just as well; he could not have lived there).
It had small room for a master of chess
and charity; an Austrian master
playing variations, in a modest
minor key, on a theme of gentleness.

What a way to go

You could be Aeschylus: touch your fire
to a line of images, beacons leaping alight
across space and time; you could go as near
to truth as words can reach; then you stroll out
and some careless fowl drops a tortoise
(I ask you), in passing, and there's your skull smashed.

But it doesn't have to be as bizarre
as that. A little too much fat will do
to harden the arteries; a little tar
silts up the lungs, and the machine won't go.
Or you could keep fit and live healthy,
and take a few years longer to die.

What a thing is a brain, after all:
how intricate its roads; what a journey
it can map out. How universal
its concerns; how timeless its memory,
housed in a structure like a Friday car
built to fall apart in a few years.

Sometimes you look out from some hill
over fields clouds roads, the smoke of houses,
over light and distance, weather and travel,
and think: who will ever guess
what moves in me; what thoughts spend
a dragonfly's day inside my mind.

Because your name doesn't need to be
Aeschylus: you could be called Fred,
and you'd still not be ready to die,
nor have answered the end for which you were made.
The problem's this: we're all of us
irreplaceable, and none of us will be missed,

and it's a waste, and what's to be done
about it? Alchemy didn't come up
with the goods; paradise is out of fashion,
and something sometime's going to put a stop
to all you are, without a by-your-leave.
Aeschylus and a few others have

the consolation of leaving a name,
and that's about all that does last,
which seems a poor prize in a risky game,
but since it appears to be the best
on offer, one might perhaps venture
quite a lot to achieve it before

the tortoise happens down. It's some motive,
at least, for gentilesse and gallantry,
and we shall not know how many live
better than they might, because they will die,
and if that seems small comfort for being dead,
no-one gave more to Aeschylus, or Fred.

In memory 1: In Morriston crematorium

In Morriston crematorium
he was burned with due decorum,

and he was scarcely thirty.
He left a wife, as they say,

and children too young to be grieved
or remember he ever lived.

He was not of decorous habits;
he should be out with his mates,

or maybe at a party,
anywhere but so tidy,

the quiet leavings of a man
stranded in Morriston.

In memory 2: A matter of scale

He left no grief on Aldebaran;
Cygnus Alpha didn't know the difference
and the long lights of the Milky Way
never paled an instant for him.

Even on his own planet
the most people did not know him;
in his own country, his own town,
his loss was a small matter.

Only in a few lives
is a void left, wider
than a town could fill, or a planet,
or the great sun Aldebaran.

In memory 3: Reallocation

No, I don't think they'll give us
a replacement. You know the boss;
if he can get three jobs done
for the price of two.... Things'll go on
quite a while with you and me sharing
whatever work won't wait; leaving
the rest on that desk. About the end
of the month, we start complaining; he'll find
someone downstairs to do the audit,
the PAs get more letters to write,
and that's Ian sorted. In a week
or so, they'll amend the office phonebook
and send a notice round; you wait
till you see his name, with 'delete'
against it; that's when you know
he's really gone. It's like an echo,
I always think: someone's been amended,
ended.

In memory 4: Closing up

Things close up at different speeds: the space
you smash through the water with a stone
scarcely defines its edges before it's gone,
poured into; smoothed over featureless.

Or take out a rock-plant in summer
and watch the others ease into its room,
breathing out; making themselves at home,
till you could never put it back there,

because 'there' 's gone. And then a bike
skids, and a man is taken out,
and the edges of the long jagged cut
in people's lives feel so raw; look

so far apart, you'd think he would be missing
for ever, but they make new habits,
rearrange their world in a way that fits
one person fewer. That's the saddest thing,

when you can't see any more in your mind's eye
what used to go where the space used to be.

Magnolia

That time when trees, in particular,
are what they can be; bloom held close
still in a clenched fist of promise,
teasing you to guess at shape and colour,
nothing gives so little away in spring
as this tree, its wrought-iron ribs lifting

into an empty cup, curved space
where a tree will happen. Perhaps memory
and foreknowledge colour it for me,
invest it with quiet desperate grace,
or maybe it just is like that.
The others come discreetly; don't wait

for almond to flower, you'll be there all week,
but take your eye off this, and tomorrow
it's covered in wax candles with a glow
of warmth inside the whiteness, the like
of a young girl's skin, or an eggshell
full of some bird's life ready to spill.

And the first wind that blows, the first shower
slaps them loose; brings all that brightness down.
If the sun shines, a few days sees them gone;
even girls and birds have more staying power
than they do. The tree, iron again,
locks in its secret beauty, each year's pain.

Rockbreaker

Your name is saxifraga sanguinea:
you are a mossy mat of green rosettes
with small red flowers on a fragile stem.
You prise apart rock's fissures; your root fits

any crack, and there's nowhere you can't grow.
Tear off a bit of you and lay it down,
and it will take, and spread, over some years,
to push walls askew; force change on stone,

which has no answer to you, since you won't
take no. I plant your will-power gingerly;
myself, I'm a stonewaller. Your name
is blood-red rockbreaker; you worry me.

Eva and the roofers

Eva in the back garden; a ton weight
of heat two inches above her,
palpable all around in the air,
her body on the grass blinding white
in all that sun and stillness. A whistle
shrills along some thread, invisible

in the light, some spider's filament,
and touches her. She looks idly back
up the sound's thin glittering track
to a roof opposite, and the glint
in the roofer's eye. He nudges his mate
and they call something, she can't hear what,

but the general idea's obvious
and she smiles to herself, satisfied
with the sun and the tribute. She puts aside
her book; shifts accidentally on purpose
to face a little more in their direction,
loosens a strap and starts stroking lotion

into her shoulder. All three play the game
as gravely as the steps of a gavotte.
('I look to be on offer, but I'm not'.
'We've no intentions, but a man can dream'.)
The garden, the fenced territory,
protects them all, wards off reality,

for while this one barrier's in place
they can let the sun melt every other.
Sex, class, reserve, duty, danger,
all *perhaps*, all blurred at the edges,
the way even people are when light
invades them so; arrows in, to commit

with so little respect, so gently,
an undressing of shape.... They work on at
their lives, while their minds float out
on an ocean of possibility.
They're singing; their skins drink sun; glow
from inside; they'll all burn tomorrow.

147

It's the magic number: seven more
than black despair, and that last black
has to be the hardest. He poises
his cue, and we all feel sick

with certainty: he won't make it.
That black is every job interview
we failed; every final step
we tripped on. It's every no

we heard when we needed to hear yes,
and it's going to happen again,
it's bound to.... There's the contact: too late now,
it's paused on the lip; we all breathe in,

and it's down, and everyone's going mad,
because destiny's taken a day off
and we've won. His laughter radiates
out at the audience; they mirror love

back to him, and everyone wants
to hold him, touch him, touch the luck,
in case it's catching. He did it
for all of us; he put down the black.

Snow-blind

I have seen real snow as fine
as that powder: there was no building
with it. You could scoop it up
man-high, but when a man tried
to firm it, then it diminished
to a mean handful.

Pain is ironed out under
the evenness that passes
for beauty, from a distance.
But it is the comfort
of sleep slicking into death,
the stuff of treachery.

Smoothness of paper ice
over a lake, translucence
of consumptive skin, blue shadows
of exhaustion, pure uncanny beauty
with a hollow back, unbroken
peace of smothering.

No-one so young should love
white; why, you were born
under the sign of the Lion
who is life and gold. Your colour
sears like sun: there's no chance
without that pain.

You belong laughing,
incandescent, like the night
you got your big break.
How came your eyes so blank,
the fun bleached out
of your face?

You rest your mind on snow
and it walls you in; shuts off
the sky; you will be snow-blind.
Oh, choose chance: touch, see, cry,
watch death's grains dissolve
in your footsteps.

A short history of cocaine abuse

The soft snow that ate your nose away
has a long history in damping down
social disorder. The first rich man
who fed it to the poor, so they say,
was the Inca, who liked his folk to stay
content with little. Then he lost his crown
to the next rich man, the Spaniard, who kept on
the good custom that from day to day
made them want less; killed their appetite.
The next rich man, up in Texas, used it
to pay his road-gangs; a happy workforce
being good for business. And the next, of course,
got rich through you, who paid his price and bought
what he chose to sell, as a good peasant ought.

Tulips

The tulips named for your home town
bloomed well for me this May.

The weather was kind to them:
no wind bowed them down,

and though for a long while they lay
under snow, they came through;

they were winners. They did their name
honour; they had shape and class.

They were not unlike you,
without the pain and the weakness

that make us care so much more
for a man than for a flower.

Sometimes

Sometimes things don't go, after all,
from bad to worse. Some years, muscadel
faces down frost; green thrives; the crops don't fail,
sometimes a man aims high, and all goes well.

A people sometimes will step back from war;
elect an honest man; decide they care
enough, that they can't leave some stranger poor.
Some men become what they were born for.

Sometimes our best efforts do not go
amiss; sometimes we do as we meant to.
The sun will sometimes melt a field of sorrow
that seemed hard frozen: may it happen for you.

Torturers

So the grandmothers walk, softly, but their black
outlines are hard in the sun, to the big house
of the president, and they demand the children
of their dead children. In voices like ash,
white and brittle, they explain that the torturers
from the last regime, when they had quite finished
playing with someone, and put them away
for good, would not infrequently find
infants left over,and would take them
home to their wives: loot.

The president is a humane man,
and not a little intimidated, besides,
by the vast loss frozen in their faces,
and he says, certainly he will try to find
what's theirs. (To bring the torturers to account
is proving beyond him; where's the evidence,
the witnesses are dead, and anyway
he'd lose half the army.... But to give back
the old women's grandchildren is justice,
for once, at a bargain price.)

So here and there, in a comfortable house
in the suburbs, some boy tries out
a new name on his tongue. The man
he has been calling father forced the screams
from his father; planted the electrodes
in his mother.... And carried him home
to feed; play with. He tries saying: torturer,
but fails, because, when you come down to it,
torturers are human like any other men,
and this man loved him.

She was nineteen, and she was bored

She was nineteen, and she was bored
with being a kitchenmaid, cleaning a house,
being nobody. She joined the murderous crew
of mediocrities out on the loose

after revenge. They gave her a uniform
and high black riding-boots; no housemaid's gear,
and a whip, and enough authority
to look in most faces and see fear.

She was head wardress; she had the word,
people lived or died at her option,
and mostly died, because, given power,
she overdosed on the exhilaration

of misusing it, of seeing her betters
at her boots: where's your brains now, eh,
your education, your class, your fancy job,
your money? She spent five years on a high.

She could have followed other roads to fame:
she might have been a heroine, a Joan,
she might have been noted for character
or wit, or courage, or compassion,

if she'd been intelligent, large-minded,
but she was neither; she was a failure
born and bred; an ignorant slut, which didn't stop her
being dissatisfied, taking what adventure

she saw. She was hanged young, as she deserved,
it's no excuse that she did what we might.
Those who made her world are still in business:
the likes of her are no nearer the light.

Penguins at Robben Island

You could not help but feel for them; trammelled
in the oil, so fumbling suddenly
in the element where they were apt to be.
Anyone would want their sentence repealed.

Now on the rocks where the guests wait,
a little gingerly, for release,
it is not they who seem any way tactless;
nothing so proper as their shuffling gait

on the land that suits their rare make
so ill; shackles their skills. They leave sidelong,
glance back, look for something to go wrong
at every step. Then when the waves speak

their bodies' language; when, unbelieving,
they learn the use of freedom again,
that's a sight to ease any man.
To see the dispossessed, living ...

in the right enjoyment of all they can be,
must be the next best thing to being free.

Because

Because our police are not averse
to setting dogs on scared working-men,
we should complain loudly when yours cut loose
with whips and guns, smiling through your pain.

Because we can be turned from any place
where our masters don't wish us to go,
our gorge should rise when you show your pass,
as if we were humiliated, too.

Because rich are so estranged from poor
that they might be of another nation,
we should flinch when your short-sighted neighbour
rebuffs you out of incomprehension.

Because things aren't yet that bad here,
we should reflect that they might grow worse;
that your rulers aren't subhuman either,
and might once have been turned from their course.

There are invasive plants: you let them in
a corner of the garden, and the root
runs underground; its nature is not seen
till it takes over: tyranny is like that,

suffer it a little, it will soon grow.
To rate your freedom cheap lowers the price
of ours: what we think good enough for you
is what will be good enough for us.

Babel (1894-1941?)

He took it all in.
the precise key of the woman's screech
on the mail coach, the latest slang
from Moldavanka, the spiel
of the NEP traders. Then he distilled it;
salt, sweat and all the forty flowers
of Odessa's autumn, rendered down

to a few words.
A hundred pages of drafts
for one story; then he'd sift through
and discard every word that wandered
from the target. 'A story's finished',
he said, 'when the only words left
are those you can't do without.'

Surely in the camp
where he was so monstrously consigned
his ear was open for some trick
of speech, some tale with a twist.
Surely, if he had to etch them
in permafrost, there exist somewhere
the drafts of one devastating page.

They are no fools, these gods,
these little power-misers; they know
what the tower of truth uses
for mortar. When it climbs too high
for their liking, they strike quickly; crumble
this dangerous matter, language, and see
how all comes tumbling down.

I am Roerek

I am Roerek: I was king
of a little scrap of Norway;
large or small, I would not part
with what I had.

I fought a man whose luck
swallowed mine; he blinded me,
but being a good Christian,
he wouldn't kill me,

just kept me about his court,
where I spent my spare time
earnestly attempting his life.
After the third try

he said: don't you ever give up?
and shipped me to Iceland.
I stayed a winter with this man
and that: we always quarrelled.

Now I lie under a hill,
hear the muffled wind shifting
over the grass; uneasy,
like the sea in a shell.

I am the only king
to lie in a land too stubborn
for kings; an edgy country.
It suits me well,

for I am one who would not
co-operate; tailor my wants
to fit reality. Roerek: king
and cosmic nuisance.

Of the lady whose museum is in Bamburgh

In your museum I can never find you,
not quite. Your pink dress proves only
that there was some five foot three
of whoever you were. It looks wrong
on the model; it should lie casually
over a chair, as if you'd just
stepped out of it.

People have wanted to encase you
before now. A woman lived much
behind glass, safe from dust and danger,
until one day, not long after dawn,
you smashed the fist of your great spirit
through the case, and launched yourself
on an ocean dark with chance.

And afterwards, when they all knew
the way to your door, few found you in.
You were not there for the newspapers;
the showmen could make no show of you:
too much class. Everyone who painted you
got you different: they're all here, the pictures
you stepped out of.

Nor could the suitors get to you:
you didn't want to know, nor
to be known. There could be but one end
to such reticence; it is no surprise
that you should, so young, give life
itself the slip. In only one place
can I see you,

your boat: those few planks of wood
flanking the space you filled
with the certainty of yourself:
a seaman's daughter, at home
in empty places, and who chose,
elusive grace, to be encountered
only in her absence.

Olaf the Quiet

Snorri Sturlusson's great chronicle
doesn't have a whole lot to say
about this king: inherited Norway
from his father, who couldn't sit still
while there was a neighbour to be hammered
or any rival asking to be dead.

(Over-reached himself at long last
by Stamford Bridge.) And what does Olaf do
but sit at home; doesn't even go
on the yearly trip to lay Denmark waste.
No revenge for his father; no adventure
in foreign lands; doesn't the man want honour?

Saga-wise, he does not rate reams;
one can but guess how those rated him
who did not go to war in his time.
It isn't many kings who earn names,
and fewer still like his: Olaf of peace,
quiet Olaf; Olaf who minded his own business.

Three epitaphs:

Skeggi

He was the bastard son
of Grettir the great outlaw;
his father's saga spares him
a sentence: 'At fourteen
he was the strongest of his age
in the north; he seemed like
to be a remarkable man,
but he died at seventeen
and there is no saga about him.'

Mary Renault

You will surely find a good welcome
where you are gone, for your acquaintance
was of the widest, limited neither
by convention of time, nor place, nor manner.

Epitaph of an impecunious publisher

(for K. A. Perryman, who is very much alive)

My earthly quest was one long search for funds;
remorselessly I tracked down marks and pounds
to turn them to the service of the word.
Through my endeavour, men's voices were heard
in lands they never knew, which at the audit
of time shall be accounted to my credit.
But Death's a creditor won't be delayed;
for all my blandishments, he must be paid
his due at last, and turn my last page over.
The issue that appeared under the cover
of my poor mortal flesh is out of print,
and here it lies, lamented, but still skint.
There'll be a heavenly edition yet,
if God provides the cash to get it set.

Railway signals

(Welsh Industrial & Maritime Museum)

This is a good place for those things to wait
whose use is over. It ends a wide street
going nowhere: artery of the failing trade
whose handsome derelict buildings were left stranded
by the ebb-tide; banks, exchanges,
chandlers, all quietly minding their lost business.

Inside the museum, the old machines
wear fresh paint: They still work; piston-engines
drive nothing round, running smooth as ever,
pulleys lift air, boilers supply power
to nowhere in particular. Outside,
a pilot cutter settles in the weed

within sight of the sea. The tide's out;
between the moorings, wooden piles jut
from the mud, each bearing a railway signal.
Nothing about them is exceptional
but their place; caught out here so far
off the rails, they look a little spare,

at a loss even, but so do most
of the exhibits, for they *are* lost
in a special way. The use is gone, you see;
it isn't like Roman jewellery
or suchlike, for that could be in use
again; the owner's dead, not the purpose.

But what's here is as far obsolete
as only modern industry can get.
What it did is being better done,

or not at all. A discontinued line,
last week's Top Thirty, last year's video game.
It moves aimlessly in the same dream

as the facades of the dead businesses,
staring up the street with their empty eyes
at the new houses for the new people.
Things have moved on; things are unsentimental
like that. You can't force the world to need you,
and if it doesn't, there's nothing much to do

except wait civilly while a layer
of nostalgia distances you, like a picture
behind glass. There will be a curious grace
to your stance, out of context and purposeless
as it is; pointing the way back,
watching the litter left in the tide's track.

Dieppe

1. Sports Day

*When the rehearsals started to go wrong,
troops landing miles off-course, boats lost
in the fog, we all told ourselves: it'll be
all right on the night. There wasn't one
of us translated those fluffed lines
into deaths.*

      There wasn't one of them
who'd seen a battle, give or take
a few officers with long memories;
they'd been training for months, making
successful landings around Portsmouth,
learning nothing.

      *We couldn't see the beach
for smoke at first: then when it cleared,
we saw a steep shelf, and a sea wall
laced with barbed wire, no-one told us
about that, and gun emplacements
everywhere, and we looked at each other
sideways, and thought Christ,
this isn't much like the Isle of Wight.*

It wasn't much like the reports
from intelligence, the ones that said
it was lightly defended, no wire,
and they wouldn't know anyone was coming.

*They were firing at us from the cliffs,
we couldn't see them; it was just a few yards
to the wall; a bloody obstacle course:*

*we were dodging, swerving, crawling,
I shut my eyes and thought: this
is unreasonable, it's dangerous, someone
could get killed. And when I looked
again, there was a whole company
just lying in the open, like they were tired
after a race; why don't they take cover,
oh Christ, they're all dead.*

                        Nine hundred
dead: another two and a half thousand
captured or wounded. Next morning
the Hamilton Light Infantry went on parade,
all ten of them; the Royal Regiment
mustered thirteen.

                    *They took prisoners
in droves; men sitting crying
among the corpses. When they marched us
away, we were so tired; throats dry,
empty inside. I remember thinking
maybe they'll give us tea and biscuits
for effort, like after sports day.*

2. Finding out

It was a great place for finding out
things you were better not knowing about.
Tracer, now; did you know it was
beautiful? You crouched and watched it lace
the sky like fireworks as you sailed in:
it was red and white, blood and bone, and men
were dying of it. The shore batteries had
the boats' range; men would jump off, wade
a few yards, then crumple. And you'd come
all that way to fight: back home
you couldn't wait for it, and this
is what it is: a boy with his eyes
hanging out, staggering up and down
the beach, cursing. Next to you, a man
starts to say something, when a hole
appears in his face. And the air is full
of a sweet heavy stench; is that how
blood smells?

        That was when some of you
discovered you weren't getting off that boat
unless the Navy boys pushed you out
at gunpoint, which some did. Once ashore,
you started finding out more and more
about yourselves; not all of it bad.
Look at the chaplain, Holy God,
just look at the chaplain, he don't care
a damn; if a man's hurt, he's there,
right through the fire. And all the days
he has to live, he will know what he was

that day; so many men will take home
that kind of knowledge; only some
would live a lot easier knowing less
about blood, and themselves, and death's face.

3. Escapers

There were those who were led away
to prison camps: tired, thirsty,
defeated, alive, safe.

And those who made it home
to hospital with a leg off,
or stomach hanging out.

Even those who stayed
on the beach: out of pain, finished
with fear for ever.

Those who went back whole,
to face again what now
they knew; it must have hurt

them to watch the escapers.
No wonder some hung back
from helping the injured

aboard; stared empty-eyed
out to sea, contemplating
their boundless prospects.

(The statistics in 'Sports Day' are taken from Ronald Atkin's *Dieppe 1942*, published by Macmillan, 1980.)

Bad weather

White's meant to happen; no doubt
in such deliberation, hour on hour
of silence drifting down, thickening
the air, muffling the tread
of feet, the wheels of cars, stifling speed,

impeding business. By and by those cars
will leave their ventures; abandon
the road to itself. It won't be taken
for granted any more; no familiar
convenience, but the blind track of danger.

Left to the snow, and its own devices,
white will silt it up; freeze hard
and treacherous under the gentleness.
There'll be no way in to work tomorrow;
no boss demands more deference than snow.

It leans heavy on the wire; telephones
hold their tongues; then the pipes freeze
and school's out. The plan's becoming clear;
something up there, if you ask me,
finds the world unconscionably busy.

The white edict runs, more or less,
there shall be no moving about
from place to like place; no work done
that need not be; no *doing*, in brief,
you are all free to go about your life

as you would if you only had the time,
time to think, time to take stock
of things. There's all the time in the world,
but don't be too scared; before you hit
screaming point, they will unlock the white.

Telescope

It showed us a collage of galaxies,
swirls of milk splashed on the dark,
and each arc studded with too many stars
for comfort, at least for mine. Because when you think,
for a moment, of so immense a number,
it's a racing certainty that somewhere

out there, someone else is thinking,
someone that lives and dies as we do
and never knows us. We see his star
six hundred years before he was born,
and all the time, he is watching the space
where we will be alive, one of these days.

And it's not 'someone' either, but a host
of someones. Maybe it's a party
going on out there; regular traffic
between the worlds; and us, as it were,
off the bus routes, at the wrong end
of all the towns. I need a friend

somewhere around Epsilon Eridani,
and you; you're hankering for a pen-pal
circling Barnard's star. We link hands
in loneliness, but our thoughts radiate.
We're too close, it seems; we can see where
it hurts, but we can't help each other.

Saga patterns

In some, the families
twist together like the swift ribbons
of streams; the action leaps
and glitters on the rocks; gathers
power and mass; slows down
as it follows the known course
of fate out to the distance
of the estuary.

Some are like weather.
Into a calm day edges
a scud of cloud – a lawsuit,
maybe, or a man's temper –
and suddenly the sky's
a great throat shouting, a gale
of killings, till the land's washed
clean: an exhausted stillness.

They are the patterns
a land and a people made,
coming together. The crops' patchwork
on the slopes, the weather-whorls
etched in the faces; a land
and a people growing from aloneness
to oneness, weaving the cloth
of community, shaping each other.

A shipwrecked Inuit learns Gaelic from a Hebridean

When he comes in, he smiles; waits for your face
to answer him, then reaches out
to touch your shoulder. You speak
the name he calls himself: Mac Cruimein;
his face lights and he nods, says it slowly
for you to get the sound right. His names
for things are softer than yours, and they blur
at the edges; change shape on his tongue
all the time. The one who keeps the fire,
who goes softly in and out with food,
the one you call *arnuk*, he calls her *ban*
and *bean* and *bhean*.... At first, you didn't guess
they were the same word; now, you wonder
by what law they change. His language
is like a code to you; you file
his words away against your own, translate
each time you listen. Meanwhile
you read what you can: the different tones
of his voice; gestures; the gentleness
in his hard hands. You are becoming fluent
in him; you know what makes him laugh,
what weather worries him, what way
he has to make a living. His woman
tends your wound; already you're beginning
to think of her as *ban*; it sounds natural
because he says it. The time is not far
when you will feel the word shift on your tongue
by no law, except what rings right
to you, as it does to them. Their soft speech
will shape your thought; change the appearance
of things you knew. And your old words,

filed away, will stiffen; grow unhandy
on your tongue, if you don't take care
of them. It's hard to keep a language
without you see it on a man's face.

(Suggested by an (imaginary) incident in a short story by Farley Mowat.)

Framed

Never saw him but in the frame
of his sister, the delicate old maid,
my great-aunt, dusting off neatly
his sardonic sepia likeness,
putting him into words —
her own, of course.

'Too much mouth, too much temper,
a black look on him.
He took his gun after a girl
who wouldn't have him; then married
on the rebound, left his wife
like luggage, and off to Canada...'.

Leaving his face in an oval
of glass and thin silver,
his character in the keeping
of his sister, a cryptographer
by trade; leaving her also
the pictures he made.

Water-colours, unutterably
careful, lakes and landscapes
captured in a fine mesh
of lines, pastel-washed, distant,
they posed in their dark frames
testifying quizzically

to the tender hand and eye
of a violent loudmouth,
a man faintly amused
by a new-fangled camera,
no black look on him
that it could catch.

Memoirs of a Dutch tulip merchant

1636 was the great year...
looking back on it now, I can see that.
The first bulbs came in around the turn
of the century, and even then, they cost:
they were so beautiful, like coloured lilies,
and so new, but they were just a fashion,
really, until the war, 1618:
traffic all to hell, and the imports
weren't getting through; that put the prices up
like no-one's business. I remember I sold
a single *Semper Augustus* – in '31,
I think it was, the year the Austrians
burned Magdeburg – for thousands: everyone
wanted *Augustus*. It had a white ground
striped with crimson and iron; the more broken
the colours were, the more it was worth.
Of course, I hardly ever saw the things
in flower. I've bought bulbs in the ground,
sight unseen, and sold them the same day,
and seedlings that wouldn't bloom for seven years,
just a promise of beauty, and men
would mortgage their homes for it, oh yes,
and more, in '36. One man bought
a *Viceroy* with all his possessions,
even his bed: an *Admiral Liefkens*
went for five thousand florins, and *Augustus*
you couldn't lay your hands on. I bought one
for thirteen thousand, and sold it for that
plus a coach and horses. That year, winter
went on for ever. I don't know how many
of those bulbs froze in the ground; plenty
of people froze above it. And the next spring,

the Government cracked down on speculation
in tulips, and we all caught a cold.
There they all were, the *Admirals*, the *Emperors*,
worth damn all except beauty, like their owners,
who weren't mostly admirals or emperors.
I was better off than most: I still had
the coach and horses.

Crusaders

Before I went, I wrote a song;
as I recall, it said something like this:
if any woman sins, she'll do it with
a coward, for all the good men are gone.
What I meant, of course, was that I'd left
a woman, and I was pig-sick with jealousy.

I went with my mate Guy; he'd left
a woman too: she loved him, which was more
than mine did. All the way out, he hurt:
he'd gone because a gentleman had no choice.
He cried one night: I wanted to hold him,
but we'd neither of us have understood.

Out East, we met this German: Hartmann
his name was; he was the oddest ever.
He wanted to die, to join his dead pal;
to tell the truth, I think he probably
was a sodomite, but I didn't hate
them so much any more; there were a few

out there, and they all fought the same
as we did. Anyway, this fellow
ran at swords, under horses' hooves;
every arrow-storm, up he popped
for a target, and they all missed him...
that's how it goes sometimes. Guy took a girl

from a town we sacked, and learned some Moorish;
he told me once he wasn't sure the Church
had the right of it. A stray shot killed him,
just before the truce. I carried him
back to the girl: we cried and made love.
She really missed him; I was quite surprised.

Then, back home, Madam in her castle
wants me to play the damn game again...
*'It's a pity, lady, that you wasted
the time your face was a flower,
play-acting'*.... The oaths followed me out:
the first honest words I'd heard from her.

Peat bog burial: Luneburg Heath

Two men in a shallow grave, though it held them
so many years. Their people buried them
out of sight, alive, for shame,
but they came back to light.

Tacitus tells us this was the use
for three criminals: the coward,
the traitor, and those who led
an unorthodox love life.

Which kind these were may be deduced
from their having been buried
together; also from the circumstance
that, by all indications, they would seem to have died
kissing.

An even worse way to go

He lies and waits for death to come near,
since mercy's face is masked, and medicine
is handed at arm's length. Which of his kin
would kiss him: which friend share
his sheets? His gaunt face is the fear
that walked the plague years, when the vermin
left the ships, and love wasn't in,
and those died who thought first of another.
He never knew there was so much space
as the vast black hole of aloneness
where he lies collapsed. He used to favour
casual contacts, brief warmth: he avoided
sleeping alone, in the short time he had
before he'd have to sleep alone for ever.

Pharisees

It was a magazine article
by some academic, deprecating
the way his neighbours named their houses.
Holly Grove, and not a sprig in sight;
Well Combe (is this, he enquires
over his spectacles, meant to be a pun?)
Raymar he can't even guess at,

but certainly it shows little respect
for the spirit of place, the house
that will be there when today's tenants
are gone with their dreams of escape
to Shangri-La, their longing to live
by a Larksbrook, their 'lower-middle-class urge
to personalise their place'.

I thought: you smug superior sod
giving thanks in the temple for your taste;
if Raymond and Margaret feared so much
to be nowhere, that they stamped their place
Raymar, they never meant to bind you.
You can look up the deeds, find out
the old name; should be simple

for a smart-arse. Then you can enjoy
being authentic, conserving the pure truth
of a house.... And when you've done caring
for the bricks, you might waste a thought
on Raymond and Margaret and their terror
of the dark. (Like me, here in the temple
giving thanks for my charity.)

He was a man of his word

He was a man of his word:
you could say no more
for his morals than that.
He would not think twice
to stabbing his best acquaintance
in the back, but if he promised
otherwise, he would perform it.

It could be well seen
how chance kept shaping him,
hunted as he was;
how the humour twisted
and turned black. He had a smile,
when it was seen, of rare sweetness:
it always reached his eyes.

His mind was lean and devious,
scanning possibilities
like any hawk its prey.
He could have been great,
given some small difference
in the universe; he still was
great of his kind,

though it was a criminal kind.
He was an outlaw to rank
with the greatest, with Gisli
and Grettir, like them betrayed
by loneliness. Nor was he less
for that his hideout was not
on a map, but in the pages

of a script. He lived and died
in his way, more than many

that have a body to their name,
and if I mourn him, it doesn't mean
I don't know fact from fiction, only
that reality happens in odd places
and comes in more wrappings than one.

A modest request

I don't ask much: just wish I could have been
Christopher Marlowe; cried the great lines
at a stunned audience dizzy and hurting
from the wordfire, senses shot to hell,
wondering how words could be so violent.
'See, see where Christ's blood streams in the firmament.'

Just wish I'd been half as dangerous,
as quick, as insufferable to all
who didn't like to be pricked into thinking:
just wish I could have been so awkward
to satisfy; so restless after knowledge.
'That like I best that flies beyond my reach.'

Of course, I would have modified the lifestyle;
blasphemed in private, left the boys alone,
kept out of knife fights, watched my words,
not that they would have needed much watching:
I see they would have discomposed no man.
'What is beauty, saith my sufferings, then?'

Cameraman

You must see all suffering,
all cruelty, all injustice, all pain:
you must fix your eye on the starving,
the tortured and the executed: you
must look away from nothing.

You must not turn your hand
to feed children, nor to caress
the dying, nor to defend
victims. You keep the lens
in front of your mind,

that others may reach
into pockets, knock on doors,
dig wells. You are the itch
in others; you can make them
see clear, if only you watch

exactly; if you record
just what happened. Do not be tempted
to turn the camera inward:
your stricken looks are no concern
of the public's. They need the word

on what you saw, not how
you felt. It is they who must feel
they saw it; they were there; so
involved, they condemn somewhat
the remote likes of you.

Last words of a once-proud Lady on her deathbed

(From the German of Simon Dach: 1605-1659)

Poor bag of worms: but a few weeks are gone
since I walked straight and supple as a deer,
greeted by many friends, honoured and fair,
and now I lie stretched out, all skin and bone.
Was this the thing I once hung gold upon?
My limbs waste, and my sight is just a blur.
I stink, friend: hold your nose and don't come near.
Oh Christ, how is my arrogance brought down!
Come ladies; come young folks: make me your glass;
learn here the worth of beauty, pride and class.
You see my life is done, and I must go.
Farewell and know yourselves; live prudently,
remember what a fright death made of me.
I do but lead the dance: you're coming too.

Rhymes

(From the German of Friedrich von Logau)

I like to rhyme, but never lit upon
as good a rhyme as woman makes with man,
as body makes with grave, pocket with pence,
wine with my stomach, life with non-violence,
or, most of all, death with an easy conscience.